HOMELAND & OTHER POEMS

POEMS

For Alberto,

Whose brother I have met — and so, I have met by default!

That we meet soon to talk poetry and all that!

Best wishes,

Ogaga

2 Sept. 1999
Lagos

Kraftgriots

Also in the series (POETRY)

Sunday Okpanachi: *A Song for Inikpi*
Ada Ugah: *Colours of the Rainbow*; winner, 1991 Association of Nigerian Authors (ANA) poetry prize.
David Cook et al: *Rising Voices*
Sesan Ajayi: *A Burst of Fireflies*
Akomaye Oko: *Clouds*
Olu Oguibe: *A Gathering Fear*, winner, 1992 All Africa Okigbo prize for Literature & Honourable mention, 1993 Noma Award for Publishing in Africa
Nnimmo Bassey: *Patriots and Cockroaches*
Okinba Launko: *Dream-Seeker on Divining Chain*
Onookome Okome: *Pendants*; winner, 1993 ANA/Cadbury poetry prize
Uba Ofei: *Beyond Fear and Fury*
Abiodun Ehindero: *Response of the Dead*
Uba Ofei: *After the Fire*
Nnimmo Bassey: *Poems on the Run*
Ebereonwu: *Suddenly God was Naked*
Tunde Olusunle: *Fingermarks*
Joe Ushie: *Lambs at the Shrine*
Chinyere Okafor: *From Earth's Bedchamber*
Ezenwa Ohaeto: *The Voice of the Night Masquerade*; joint winner, 1997 ANA/Cadbury poetry prize
George Ehusani: *Fragments of Truth*
Remi Raji: *A Harvest of Laughters*; joint-winner, 1997 ANA/Cadbury poetry prize
Patrick Ebewo: *Self-Portrait & Other Poems*
George Ehusani: *Petals of Truth*
Nnimmo Bassey: *Intercepted*
Joe Ushie: *Eclipse in Rwanda*
Femi Oyebode: *Selected Poems*

HOMELAND & OTHER POEMS

POEMS

kraftgriots

Kraft Books Limited
University of Ibadan
Post Office Box 22084
Ibadan
Oyo State, Nigeria.

FIRST PUBLISHED 1998

ISBN 978–2081–95–7

(Kraftgriots is a literary imprint of
KRAFT BOOKS LIMITED)

FIRST PRINTING, JULY 1998

Dedication

For my mother, Augusta
who heard the first poem:
Ọmaha 'gbe ti t'ọkpako?—

Will the child
Not become a man?

Acknowledgements

Most of the poems here have been published before in magazines, journals, anthologies and newspapers, including the following: *The Guardian*. *The Times Review* (DAILY TIMES), *ANA Review* (Association of Nigerian Authors), *Okike*, *Voices from the Fringe* (ed. H. Garuba, Malthouse, 1989), *Ase* (Calabar Poetry Club), *Stand*, *Opon Ifa Review*, *Praxis*, *Poetry International*, the bi-lingual anthology, *und auf den Strassen eine Peste (ed.* Uche Nduka, Horlemann, 1996).

The author wishes to thank Obiora Udechukwu for permission to reproduce his painting, *No Water*, used for the cover illustration.

Contents

Page

tomorrow's songs

I

today's song

Would you know why his poems
never mention the soil or the leaves
the gigantic volcanoes of the country that bore him?

Come see the blood in the streets
come see
the blood in the streets
come
see the blood in the streets!

— *Pablo Neruda*

For art's sake

We shall shun pain
and write lyrics of the ear.

We shall write only
— the redness of setting suns
on wonders of rolling seas
— the greenness of forest leaves
and the songs of dwelling birds
— the sweetness of women's eyes
and the adventures of stubborn loves.

We shall roam the full earth
and see no pain on our paths
and no evil in men's hearts.

For art's sake, we shall shun
pain, and write lyrics of the ear.

14 October, 1987

Untold terrors are gathered...

Untold terrors are gathered
in her only one song.

She recalls vainly, the deep
promise of children
whose naming ceremonies
called forth the joys
of the neighbourhood
and festooned her every evening
with the well-fed sleep
of healthy days.

But untold terrors are gathered
in her only one song...

Mother, when flowers and balloons
mock the terror of the days
to give unceasing laughter
to downtown homes,
when you recall in flaming anger
the anguish of today
in your one song of pain,

Refrain it with the thunder
of a rain-starved sky
set on his season
of waters and growth
and the cleansing of a dusty earth.

1989

No water

(to Obiora Udechukwu)

When the sky claps
to call down rain

rush out your bowls
till roofs dry their brows

when you turn taps
and fetch full rust
each day in a year

do you gather maidens
to balance pots on heads
to seek out streams

or uproot your home
to resettle by rivers?

When the sky claps
to call down rain

rush out all vessels
and pray for everlasting rain.

7 December, 1987

Sanitation day dream

In her dream
a bulldozer came for her shack
paused in the heat of argument
took a dignified look around
considered it beneath its time
and matching her children's wails
with its muscular worksong
cut off her breasts
with glistening iron teeth.

And the children
in line with new sanitation habits
(which bulldozers enforce)
sought to stop her fast fading breath
by heaping sand on her fatal wounds.

1990

Driftwood

Driftwood, dead hyacinth
or the emptied pack
of Benson & Hedges
cast out carelessly by a sad sailor
may sail with the current
as watercraft,
all of which is commonplace
nothing to move waves
or feet of flesh
from their race to shore and grave.

But he sailed the current
his windblown belly
sailcloth of one craft
whose journey had no more need
for destination and disembarkment.
His eyes were now big enough
to find the right path, big enough
to kill the darkness of his new world,
so what would that be
in his pumped-out arms — thwarted fight?

Surely this was no commonplace
and the funeral crowd of hawker
commuter, busboy, pickpocket etc.
rushed on bridge rail
to pay last respects
to one who like them
was once flesh and blood,
now sailing to a vulture's feast—
carrying the curse of a profane world?

Perhaps we have lived too long on dunghills
to know dignity worthier than dogs' and dungbeetles'

or, put simply, the poet's
every grave marks the end of the world
urges a kinder hand to memory
than the building of gravestones
to prompt pilgrimage of tears and flowers.
So let corpses like driftwood
like slain dog on highway, live with us
to mark the rotting of living flesh.

31 August, 1991

For Onoriode

(who peeped into earth, took fright

and hurried back to life)

We are too frail to follow after you.
— Joseph Brodsky,
"The funeral of Bobo"

I

That evening, at Ughelli, when
I held you, and you hugged me too strong
for limbs hardly out of cartilage
I should have known
that what gave the hug its bear strength
was a waiting sentence of welcome and goodbye?

That evening, when you wore suppleness
even to your fingernails, and
advertised life like no billboard nor television could
I should have known
that charmed to your skin's deep allure
was not man's eye alone, but the grave's too?

What terror puts a man to melting fright
can chill a child's blood to stone.
And if a peep into earth reveals Maroko, Middle East
Chernobyl, Ethiopia, Soweto, and trees bearing warheads,
if a peep reveals justice robed in banknotes
what lullaby can a child mime to toy guns?

II

Today I know death is illiterate
and if her soothsayer read the cowries well
and hit her forehead with the spatula's true word

she would have cringed
from wrapping with stained plantain leaves
one whose mouth was yet to speak sin;

She would have known we would make your choice a battle:
out of love, you stayed your feet longer
on our hearts' languid earth — grandmother burned
her love on your fevered forehead, and sought to
fertilise her heart for your flight-timed feet
with her daily spread of ash and tears.

But we all crave happiness,
and though for every laughter
we wail twice as long
fail in strength to renounce a world
whose comforting palms are talons of pain
leaving us to mourn our weakness, and funereal courage.

1 June, 1990

She lay dying at Oshodi

You can trust the headless scream of Oshodi
to bury in its cemetery
a frothful battle for living or dying.
And if this concerned a child of twelve
watching death roll to her on rail tracks
what sympathy can come
from the raw-peppered heart of such a horde?
You can trust Oshodi to undertake
the wake of the living.

A mere girl of twelve!
She clutched the earth, begging life
in fistfuls of mud, foaming
in her feverish plea for a healing hand.
We filed past, casting half-glances
pleading in turn, impotent worlds of sorrow
where love, lacking muscle, weeps in little graves,
hurrying through the broken fence
to flee malediction in her fading eyes.

The train tolled its horn as I crossed the fence
and I wondered if she was bound for home
before the fever made a fire in her bones,
wondered if home was her deathbed of murk
where Oshodi profanes life and death.
I passed again the scene of her mortal battle
and saw the fight she waged then
as she lay dying by the railbars
hoping to pluck a ministering hand
from a crowd deader than her dying self.

I too filed past her on that day,
forced to pay last respects to one
more in need of life than mourning.

Dear girl, twined afresh by guilt
I plead breathing corpses of your mourners
in mitigation. I plead flesh that fell
with yours, leaving only rattling bones
that toll your silent cry forever
in the wilds of a headless world.

31 December, 1990

For Otamowerai

What the carpenters cut off
was not your foot, but
the hoof of sorrow. So today
you surface from the sea's sandbelly
to begin the healing of broken pots.
A praise song flutes forth from the crutch
that beat crawl-tracks when suddenly
broadways grew forests around you,
a praise song hymned to your stubborn spirit.

You are testimony to the farmer's lore:
the planted seed yields a barn.
In seasons past, the multitude of mouths
needing ceaseless morsels of life
failed to cast iron lids on your pots,
and strangers lost their fretful brows
to the laughter of a new home.
Now in mending your broken pots, you marvel
at so many gatherers of water, clay and potsherd.

With neither cane nor chalk, you teach us
worthier lessons than the dusty walls of classrooms.
Where did we, who scraped
faith to dry bones, dredge hope?—
Your convalescing palm, stretched out
to shine the sun of new life!
On steps cut into life's capricious cliff
with the bone of a sorrowed foot, we will
climb to shore to chant your valiant song.

20 May, 1991

Traces

(to Tracy Chapman)

Music is muscle, given xylophones
and a sophistication of African drums
the sort that fired warriors' blood
with hot bronze
and compelled the maxim gun.

Music is muscle...

The line you may not cross,
that builds brick walls
between colours,
the line you may not cross
with feet and skin of wood
you cross with talking drums.

Music is muscle...

They jingle false coins
and spread counterfeit hopes
beneath bleached noses, that say:
praise the smelling salts of life
only empty vessels may be filled,
name your price
we will sell our soul
and keep the shell!

Music is muscle...

On the trail of demons
you beat false paths
Tracing roadmaps to hell,
beside your shadow lurks
liar, conjurer, thief

with tongue of many roads
bearing banners that boast:
good people are our stepping stones!

But music is muscle
and if some will save their souls,
drain seas
to fight fires burning bridges
across the line,
if some will
save their souls to save themselves

We shall see revolution's whisper rumble
with the potency of drum and wind,
we shall see the tables turn
two legs burnt out
with the fire of fertile fury.

1 September, 1991

Our eyes are born again

Daily, our eyes are born again
to sorrows wider than the world:
the cooking pot is home of spiders
and lizards are landlords of the kitchen
affirming the death of fire in countless nods,
who braves the market place
drains purse and heart
for a spoonful of salt.
The streets are alive
fighting the ghost of naira
and on a furious noonday
the sun firm in punishment
Lagos parades her despair:
a preacher with acolyte
prescribes repentance, faith and miracles
in logic needing healing,
a horde of beggars pleads death to pluck pity
and every night, my neighbours
are kept awake by their wailing children.
And you ask how life is
with them that fed on stones
in the time of little sorrows?
And you ask what hand speeds the clock
towards the rotting of living flesh?
Without the preacher's faith
I count miracles daily:
the streets still sprout life
as grave-diggers break their backs, overworked
and if daily our eyes are born again
to sorrows wider than the world
may our blood too boil anew
to chain the demons of death.

27 April, 1992

The deluge (22 April 1990)

(for G.O.O.)

Moments lived upon heartbeats of the Delta
where rivers part into oil and water
segregating stream-flow to farm neither fish nor drink,
such moments can bear a grudge thick and stubborn
like the panting roots of mahoganies.

Moments lived upon the futile till of earth
poisoned by its wealth (which runs every seam
full with oven heat of liquid gold)
so mortally wounding the laughter of barns
and harvests, in the stunned tongues of hoers,
such moments can bear a grudge prickly
and stubborn like sawblades of elephant grass.

And we see
how veins of a malarial world
overblown like abandoned cows' udders
spill their pain on what patches
of cassava soil there are
so worsening a hostility of rain floods,
of creek-invasion, with the curse of oil:
And what grudge, galled to greenness so long
avoids the deluge of split skies?

A fisherman knows the fury of windstorms,
if he turns his wounded brow round about
from the raised masts of trawlers
and finds a tyranny of faith and uniform,
how best to clear an acre of contented living
but by turning fisher of men
whose intemperate breath of acid
wear us thin to thigh bones,
how best but by flushing out of power-bunks

with same gunsmoke as rode them in atop tanks?

A map relieved of Sahelian haughtiness
lets life flourish unransomed
to the threat of a pilgrimage to the sea!
In the silences of hearts, of unspoken
feared truths, your new geography finds ovation
only that I fear how I may still share creed
with comrades who with me
are victims of the evil
that unlocked your purse—
in search of a final cure?

Earth bears the signs of a deluge
in flooded homes, farms and rivers,
even in roads closed by fallen trees,
the aftermath is pure bath
silt and litter swept to sea.

May, 1990

Song from underground

(for NANS at 10)*

Knowing the futility of sawblades against a song
they rescued their anthem with a cage
of clenched-fists. Driven from broad highways
running with the equities of their song
they found dustlaid footpaths loamier
to grow roots for iroko** heights

For questions rose sharper than arrows
to perforate learned hoods,
questions rose like tongues of fire
to lick dainty gowns
and soon enough, they found
blood filled the inkwells of their pens

And their gaze scanned the vanishing print
of books, professors' roached suits,
the leaking roofs of rabbit hostels,
streets tramped bare by job-seekers;
their gaze scanned faces
grieved darker than the smog of creaking factories

And in drama mimicked by coup-day
tank parades, street questions asked loudly
invited the bloodrain of gunmen
rusty without war, without learning
leaving each time despoliation
and judgement in the scars of whip wounds.

So they asked:

---

* National Association of Nigerian Students

** A majestic tropical rain forest tree, seen as the king of the forest for its height, size and splendour.

He whose days have seen so much blood
will he tremble before palm oil?
Limbs that ascended mountains
and descended
over the dizzier heights of corpse and grave,
will they quake at the despot's throne?

A decade of songs sung from senate floors
to streets and cells, called out the chorus
of tree branches in a May of ripening anger,
and bringing out the song-cage
defiantly square in the broad highway, they declared
the iron pledge to give teeth to their song.

26 June, 1990

Red rain

Upon the faded bones of ancient miners
from the dark tunnels of coal
I blow a song of rain
now my sky hangs tremulous
with the burden of a red cloud;
a song that refrains: remember, oh rainmakers
    your blood too has the same manner
    of flowing easily into sand or sea
    like the one you rush from hearts
    with the hot barrels of guns.
Upon Iva Valley, the argument was mined
to equality of blood, and a race-trounced tongue
decreed a hierarchy of blood with colour.
And it rained upon a patient valley
her majesty's colonial as rainmaker.

The red drum sounded
they could no longer bear their country:
their valley-chilled blood
was too hot and sudden.
Towns villages households
turned eager abattoirs,
to escape the rabble of warcries
war-profiteers fled tables for trenches
and dyed wearing apparels
in weeping colours of infant blood,
whoever looked up was silenced by the rain.
To keep the thrones of power
in their rooms of lucre
they killed thirst drinking from their own wounds.

Too many guns and soldiers
idle without wars of honour
trained their rifles upon bank-vaults, turning

the country battlefield and shooting range:
at midnight yesterday, thirteen were shot
a general came on air at dawn
to whip applause for easy crime,
today, sixty-two were battered to bone
hugged to their stakes of sand
for trying the secret of gunpowder,
and when the country flowed into street
corners, anger written on tree leaves
it rained, with generals as rainmakers.

Held beneath a red cloud
everything wears a red mark:
    it glistens in the tears of child and mother
    flutters on wind-chased leaves
    flows in street drains
    spreads on heated asphalt
    and swims in the streams,
    it marks the general's boots
    blowing sirens on his staff-car.
Come into the street, and see
how a heavy rain turns it red
come into the street, and hear
the fading boast of a general:
"blood will flow" if they protest again!

Today, all the bleeding till the 'morrow,
let all that is stained
wear its red mark for remembrance
till the cleansing hour
when street corners shall yield up their mice
an army of sponge and water,
it shall rain soaps and salts
upon the stains of my country,
it shall rain to sweep to sea
the soot and smoke of burnt powder
And remember, oh rainmakers
that your blood too has the same manner

of flowing easily into sand or sea,
remember the rain of those you bleed!

23 January, 1991

Poem to the child of my time

Because biology is neither meat nor milk
and life demands the strengthening of bone
you will find mother's breast, and
eat her daily portion of grief;
Because home is not a house for men alone
and animals need their warm bed and kitchen
you will learn love for all life, trained
in early years to live with roach and reptile;
Because birth is not cotton for a naked back
and fashion forbids fig leaves outside madness
you will find a way to clothe your ribs
in a one-robe wardrobe sewn to your skin;
And because after birth there is thirst for water
love and living, all of which cost far above
the labour of nine months, you will
drown thirst in the kindness of waste water.
But because it was easier for mother and father
to labour once and reap you, than
tell from frowning farms and factories
whether biology is not a plague;
Because the world has moved without rest
from beginnings deeper than the origins
of air and water, and immeasurable age
now makes her sleep night and day;
Because the eye that gave warmth in tender fires
to free men from the coldness of stone
and paste a growing chart where the blood pumps,
And hands that worked cassava and corn.
that bellies be not a grave for the guts
to ward off funerals of the living
Have left the world to itself
and governments, politicians, soldiers
multiply God, guns and greed.
where a child and his tree play too peacefully

Making you begin at birth battles of sword
and sickle against enemies that are legion,
and because your head finds no pillows
besides the rocks of your battles;

You ponder the world upon crying seas
whose wounded waters suffer
the navigation of sorrows round the brow,
upon famished roads whose roadcamps
are the many boulders, bleeding you
to final sadness, so that you will be either
Paul or Pagan before God, whom you ask again
and again: Is satan so strong
it takes all this time and tears
to take him to his promised hell?

19 September, 1992

The soldier has a fine head

(a song for politicians)

The soldier has a fine head
caps sit well on it
hats fitted for civil robes
taunt mirrors with approaching time

His smiles bare the fangs of hell
in every dance of his wondrous leg
magical even with a swollen foot,
his mouth, a highway,
trafficks mountains of strange sorrows

His shoulders, broadened
for all the stars and swords
of "Marshall of the World"
twinkle with blind stars, crossing
swords with enemy shadows

And his voice, ah, his voice!
a true commandant's, turns
his men tail or parrot
with the creaking of a rusty gun,
when he speaks on television
the lights go out!

But where are the politicians?

He spoke again yesternight
and lengthened a night of serpents,
because words are vapour in his mouth
he casts veils with promises

But where were politicians yesternight?

They say they shat in their briefs
stunned to jelly by his voice—
their "people" were far away in villages
retelling fables of a greedy king;

They were busy cleaning up
to be fit for their wicker parliament
which he broke with many guns
to break the lock of law and order.

And they say:
now the parliament is full of holes,
words may enter and freely go out
to save an armoured throne

But where are the politicians?

> The hourglass too slow to measure time
> the world counts in seconds
> But what heights does my world seek
> marking time with prison bars?
>
> Eyes that should span the sky
> to feed its thundering mouth
> with a cannon cry of renewal
> peep into moneyed places
> blind to bales of excess death.
> Oh house of crumbling pillars!
> tongues that should speak your oracle
> congregate in barracks
> whimpering prayers to rust-iron.

11 December, 1992

When I hear martial songs

Tomorrow, when I hear martial songs
I will smart with green-cloth envy
and be guilty of this wish:

that I were a general
my stars earned not in battle fields
nor for strategies of wars won
but in the comfort of stolen power.

May my loins sire only sons
they shall be soldiers
they shall all be generals
and end my lingering envy.

10 December, 1987

Greed will kill the beast

An empty challenge lies in the streets
he comes with fanfare
in a backbone of eggshells
to stage a mock battle.

A siren is mounted on his horns
deafened by a stunning silence
he mistakes despair for unspeakable joy
a bullet-proofed convoy echoes nothing else.

Horns and hoofs mark the beast
but yearning for a human face, skinned
his siblings, cloaked his horns and took salute
"the beast! the beast!" they cried.

In the wake of his outriders' madness
a child rises from the dust
picks his tray and oranges
and swears to tear this picture off his reader.

But the beast is in the street
and neither street nor home is safe
he paves his way with loaded rifles
he needs the cover of wild fires.

He rides into all homes
fouls their waters, ransacks their rafters
and seizing a sleeping child
feasts on the family bed.

Brother! you go too far
in search of what the books say is evil
or perhaps this which billboards the streets
is too large for encyclopaedia?

The refuge of a home proves a child's sandhouse
before horns and hoofs
before sirens, guns and tanks
what is a housewife's kitchen knife?

This season, gravediggers nurse aching backs
placing adverts for relief workers
and a fear reigns
as to who shall be next to grace their graves.

Now even curses sound like prayers
the orange boy twirls his sling
and recalling David and Goliath
asks: what will kill the beast?

They now walk on the streets' bushy offsides
to save themselves from the range of gunmen
in the boiling heat of swallowed rage
they ask: what will kill the beast?

Greed will kill the beast
in his roaring lust, fastened
on a child. Deafened by his sirens,
blinded by a habit of defiance.

He will not let go his flesh
and flee the wrath of poisoned arrows
shooting from every eye,
greed will kill the beast.

December, 1990

other songs

His life was gentle and the elements
so mixed in him that nature might stand up
and say to all the world "This was a man!"

— *William Shakespeare*

...but woe unto that man by whom the Son of man is betrayed! good were it for that man if he had not been born.

— *Mark 14:21*

Mandela's mantle

Your mantle will burn bones to ash
unless shoulders are clayed from steel
upon which now hangs a race's centuries-burden,
your mantle will burn bones to ash.

They thrust upon your forehead, a lamp
its oil bartered for thrones by them
who now drown their guilt:
light our tunnel of shame, O lightbearer!

Now they queue at telephones
to savour a moment's boom of voice
keener than assault rifles, they queue
to host greatness they know not.

Twenty-seven notches carved by stonebreaking
on your face mark the return of priests
to natives, baiting now not with beads
and gin, but whitewashed thrones.

Still pride will flush my brow
when from the high shame of Mobutu,
Bokasa, Banda, Amin, Doe
and a swarm of state house generals,

I hear saints and sinners quake at voice
to utter the name Mandela! Pride will
flush me deep to accept your
welcome gift of a flaming mantle.

May, 1990

Her bed is vacant again

(for Winnie Mandela)

When finally he returned to his portion
of bed, a poem grew ecstatic and said:
Now the wedding can take place
and loneliness will no longer burn her pillow...
But her bed is vacant again...
For the stolid stones of prison
a wider gulf is burned
with burning brands of heated hope.

The union it's true was "in a time of cholera"
leaving her nurse and patient of the plague
she could not mend socks or buttons
she could not serve a favourite dish
to an evening's hungered lips, and
she lacked bedtime stories for her kids.
or she could have told of blood and crocodiles
turned Soweto's wailing streets
Jo'burg's mine-and-hostel bone-crushings
to lullabies of a peaceful night?

and her bed is vacant again...

She became tough from the plague
like the burnt bark of baobabs
to sprout new life from gnarled tissue
earning her time in crocodile teeth, bedfires
and police dogs out to sniff danger from her skin
and the fire of bones hewn to marrow
taught virtue in hatred for fellow men
who sauce appetite with human colour
forcing her who could have loved blindly
to seek beacons for her choice.

but her bed is vacant again...

In the soul-bruising anguish of deserts
we praise the hardiness of cacti
not floral splendours or perfumed tenderness:
the harmony of harps dies in thunder and mortar.
The two were pledged to a thing
wider than winds or oceans, wider
than the selves in singular joys or pains,
the two were pledged to an uneasy walk
where two roads must be right
if in separating the journey, they lead home.

So if after he returned to his portion
of bed, her bed is vacant again
let the poem rewrite itself, and say:
the wedding took place and lasts
in the colours of a new day

3 May, 1992

Sisulu's song

When they asked: what god do you serve?
We answered: one that is colour-blind
jealous of his art
who cannot bear the stroke of pagan paint
and he's served us this far, he strengthens us.

When they asked: are you gods or men?
We answered: there is a god in every fear
cast into the terror of mortal ache
poisoning reason beyond an ocean of sharks
    blind in fear, you worship this god.

Hear our song that breaks rocks
and cheers when the axe-head flies
to slaughter crocodiles at sea,
hear our song that husbands widowed homes
    and makes men gods that worship truth.

What god we serve?
Who said: lose your life to crush clay-gods
and their cannibal taste for coloured flesh,
bind it to an eternal stretch of concrete posts
    and I will make your tongue flames of street songs.

Who said: cast a vigilant eye upon the waters,
they will harden into rock
and bury a pestilence of sharks and crocodiles,
crowned with life, you shall walk ashore to your people
    then will I make you heralds of a coming day.

And he who said: I will necklace your night
with millstones and cast it into the sea
is colour-blind, seeing only
the rising shrine of common faith — our tower of strength!

23 January, 1991

Buthelezi's blues

Soon, this withered earth will ripen again
and a song learnt in broken tongue
will sing the sky in pure air, this earth
now ocean of tears and thorns, ocean
of blood and battered bone, will ripen again

and I, where will I be?

Soon, the grounds will be swept
and festooned with a risen heart
the sweat of onion, wine and ascension song
and there will be the hallowed stand
for the giant toast to fist and mettle

and I, where will I be?

Soon, the table will be set
for the breaking of bread, baked
with the flour of fallen flesh
whose buried bones till the soil, baked
with the living fire that tends the grain

and I, where will I be?

Soon, very soon, same feet that marched
against prison and poison
will march against my charnel-house
my vault of vipers, skulls and witchpowders
defiant of maim and murder

and I, what must I do?

I must throw against this surging ripeness
a bowl of fire. And garbed in my

leopard skin, with a roaming axe, make a plague.
If I cannot reverse the river
can I not poison it with its own blood?

3 August, 1992

For the soldier of umkhonto we sizwe

There under the poplar and pine
where you clean your gun, and
sharpen to quick anger, your knife
whose lips enjoy the taste of bad blood
there lurks death in the shadows, armed,
fearful of the death that dwells in you!

There, under the poplar and pine
warsongs come to you, rendered
in murdered dreams, in turbulent
elegies of deaths washed in red foam
with choruses so bitter the leaves fall
from trees out of season, so bitter!

There, under the poplar and pine
you read the age of the moon, and
arming your feet with the spring of triggers
in which a constant dream of things
far and near, cause spears to dance the nation,
you rouse your comrades to dewbath and victory.

In the absence of wife and daughter
you kiss a yellowed photograph
and hug the air where they should be
and today, by the village church, where
the choirgirl prayed and sang the praise of the army
you oiled your trigger with living water.

You walk the backstreets of your land
its corridors pursued by the dead air of colour,
your feet mark mass graves wherein lie
bones that sought love from leaping fires
fed by human faggot. Ah! terrible task, this
taming of anger to hold the heart with love.

Still the orphan's cry is mocked to death
by the bark of police dogs
the widow's bed is mourned
by a pair of workboots worn at night
by a ghost. A homeland chieftain has drunk
a sea of blood, another prepares a bloodbath.

Ah, my brother! There is terror
in this truth of guns and knives
which together with congresses of words, faith and
marching feet, will bend a murderous trigger to itself.
There is terror in the truth of Quito Quanavale
Sharpeville, Soweto, Ciskei ... terror in the truth
that must kiss and fire a gun, and kiss again!

2 October, 1992

Homeland

What are the things that grow here?
Those that grow from stone, lacking
life and root, flesh and water
things cut as caps
for the baldness of stone.

What are the things that flourish here?
Those that rise from dust, without
teeth for the nourishment of sand
things frail and fallen, that fly
with the winds in sweat and sadness.

And what are the harvests here?
Of corn crippled before teething
Of tubers poorer than the planted head
Of tomatoes rotted before ripening
Of sand and gravel, burntbush and anthills.

What are the dwelling-places?
Houses bitter like a weeping face
homes grievous like smoke-pipes
walls held up by pillars of anguish,
where lament makes bed and roof.

And how do children grow here?
Out of wombs whipped with want
and desire, they burst forth, to be
tough like street leather, sweet and hardy
like sugarcane, to learn love in safe time.

Here, we will walk the streets
where laughter is hidden in deep places
and stores cannot shut their doors
choked with hearts that bleed from gathered wounds
and you will see nothing can grow here, but agony.

3 October, 1992

You carved too close to bone, Maggie

(Being tribute to Margaret Thatcher, the butcher, no, "who does carve at the joint")

1

You carved the joint too close to bone
your knife grew blunt. When felled trees
barred your narrow path, poorly, your arms
flailed with a table knife. And cheaply
they pulled victory from your neck
stuck stiffly on a dreamed glory:
a world rid of men who would spread
the communal lard to parched tongues.

2

At the head of an oval table
your tongue of rawhide whipped ministers
with scowls, until shamed like errant children
embraced your mother's truths, or
faces turned to toes, wrote valedictory
letters. Alone you chewed laughter
between gums of shrapnel.

3

Out of the staunchness of your heart
filled with dark passions
you professed a love for Blacks, greater
than Jehovah's for his Jews:
across the British Channel, in the coloured
streets of Soweto, you dined
on a morsel of caked blood, slept
open-eyed in rainswept bantustans, marched
heartbroken on funeral trains, fed
orphans at your breast with milk snatched

from pampered pupils' rations back home.
Queen-mother of the Blacks, your tongue
sang so well the double-note song of sanctions!

4

The sun cast deep shadows on the map
you alone heard the anguished lament
from ancestral graves: Empire or Little England?
The pony on whose back
you fired finishing salvoes
at picketers, burying them with placards
in the ruins of coal mines
saddled you to the virgin lands of Argentina,
shepherding on your rod, turmoils of home,
and in the aboriginal carcass of Belgrano
hoisted your flag with primitive pride.

5

The grand columns of Downing Street
quaked with widening cracks in the wind,
it came too loud for your frail ears:
the settling of quarrels in Germany
the continental quest for communal living.
"Empire or little England...?"
And you pledged;
    I will carve at the joint
    till they bow to the blade
    and embracing my lone star
    out of the howling sky
    declare me the last legend
    of the century. All may turn
    from the evil of forbidden paths,
    not this lady, with amulets in her skirts.

6

You carved too close to bone, Maggie
to stop a night of nemesis and its rain.

Who would dare the voters' own pledge
to levy tax at the polls?
Down Downing Street, the puddles pooled
pushed out of Number 10
you drowned in ankle waters, with a silent cry.

6 August, 1990

Dance the maggie

(At Marlborough Conference '86)

She stepped into the conference hall
fortified with her mail heart
to weather a sanction craze
with a mother's tune on morals:
"Don't hurt my poor Blacks!"

She stepped out jubilating
her assets safe in iron chests
to paste her victory on employment charts.
Tonight, my wonderful lady
beat your chest with a thousand palms
your Blacks will eat their chains for dinner.

11 August, 1986

Atop the rubble of berlin wall

January threw blood in dazed eyes
those that hung hope on straw lines
watched it burn to thread
in the war-rooms of United Nations'
Inner Chambers. This time, war-talk
cheered in the warmth of back-slapping:
the bold line of East-West arm-wrestling
faded into I.W.A's ringside delight.
At tea break, tea-cups filled with oil
freshly served from Kuwait's flow-stations.
And a convocation of five, convoked
in war to nurture war
banished an era of cold armaments:
peace is aftermath of war
what use are gunsmiths
if killing is crime?

Herod's bequest is war-winner
if adults are evil, infants are devils!
Cheaper to squash the viper's eggs
than pluck his children's mouths of fangs.
And an infants' food factory
was bombed to dust.
The peace of a flaming world
lay in palms of the Pentagon
as Saddam's little devils
preceded him to hell
their tails burning
with the fire of saints.

They saw fear in splitting grains of sand
water to slake a burning throat
crimsoned in the ventured jug
its bearer losing the vital arm

to the cannibal rage of bombs.
To clear the passage of pipelines
all could be broken
bone, brick or bottle.
This was no time to search
for the crying cactus
in the evil eye of a desert storm
no time to search for the oasis
where all paths scorch searching feet.
Ghosts provoked from graves in
Nicaragua, Angola, Panama
Grenada, Chile, Libya...
burn flags of stars and stripes.

They knocked down the wall
and East crossed to West, singing
we give our seats to you
and stand to watch your pleasure
turn them footstools.
Passions of a monstrous love beginning
cast errors of the suitor
into craven image for worship
And atop the rubble of the wall
slowly quickens—
oh quaking child of trembling union—
the concrete terror of a budding century.

19 August, 1991

tomorrow's songs

A single metaphor can give birth to love.

— *Milan Kundera*

Tomorrow the rediscovery of romantic love
...all the fun
under Liberty's masterful shadow.

— *W.H. Auden*

The Beatitude

(for Omolola

(i) What the spirit enjoins

What the spirit enjoins
in the purity of untutored paths
free from the stiffness of rule-books
and duty compelling orders
must be sundered by nothing else:
the spirit judges without mirrors that make
neither worse nor better, grace or grime.

The pilgrim's road is not his pilgrimage
more of his tortured test of faith
can he dread his promised laughter
so much from his road's scare and skull
take the portent for the power
and still call the dust of his praying knees
to witness his abiding love? In what?

It must come to be asked and answered
what our hearts must shun: sin or sinners?
If love flows not in mere rain-runnels
but deep over-flowing rivers
for those needing baths to cleanse in
what heart so against the wasting of grace
will take offence and still plead love? For whom?

Let the righteous love the righteous
and the filthy-ragged the filthy-ragged.
Who will nurse the boil-infested
recoils her dainty fingers from pus!
Where vines cannot bloom for labourers'
lack of sickle space, he goes still
to plead excess love for work. To reap what?

The lantern shines best in darkrooms,
not beneath midday suns. And what
is not against the light and laughter
of hearts throbbing in common joy
of each being the other, opening
and closing to breathe curative air
is abundant life or nothing!

What the spirit enjoins
in the purity of untrodden paths
above the fearsomeness of laws and orders
must be sundered by nothing else.
Were the errors of undivined paths tied to toes
who would dare learn to walk? And be truly hurnan?

5 December, 1991

(ii) The earth you walked to me

The earth you walked to me
spans swamps and savannahs
your fertile plot of pineapples
its sweetness guarded
by thornbush.

The truths of a rising heart
defy mathematical formulas
its equations find balance
in the salted breath
of your fresh fruit mouth.

I run my forefinger
round your dewdrop face, drawing
the world in invisible paint, plain
only to you and I:
you are the world for which
clay was "tinsel" raw material.

One moment of a deepening look
into each other' eyes
till your heart awoke to a tender hand
and you quaked: "*what do you want?*"
Oh, it needed no answer
but I said: "*you, bone, blood and breath!*"

The earth you walked to me
is the pineapple's thornbush
and I exalt in its cuts and bruises,
it led your feet to my ash-house
where your lips parted
and blew alive
virgin coals needing the taste of fire.

27 January, 1992

(iii) If one looks at your face

If one looks at your face
your bosom, your waist
he will free laughter
from the teeth of crocodiles
and wash his face again.

Your eyes are the kitchen stoves
whose fires will never quench
not even in Noah's flood,
your eyes are where we may roast
stones to bread for famished mouths.

Your breast, milk-mellon multiplied
to cure the thirst of multitudes
enough for my famished mouth,
enough for my hunger-dredged gullet
I claim against tooth, nail, water.

Your waist is the continent's coast of gold,
draws envious claws to pillage,
but there, is my mine of laughter
crowned with the glitter of dust,
round it I make a fence of fire with my arms.

And when a stranger comes
beaten by streets and winds
to lay camp beneath your roofed eyes
you wash his face with his lost laughter
and kill one more crocodile from the neighbourhood.

29 January, 1992

(iv) The cock may crow thrice

The cock may crow thrice, crow
till it be sore in the throat, till
its comb burns with fire, and
each feather a sword, cuts
a treacherous night's thieving hand

my love will be surer
than the night's bleeding star.

And till dawn shames the swords!
The leopard cannot shed its spots
so cannot Christ his nail spots
the tiger cannot shed its stripes
so cannot Christ his whip stripes

my love is surer
than a sweet and sour prophecy.

I count a long night
beyond a disciple's tears
and follow the bitter road of the cross,
I count the jeers, fears and cheers

of a heated crowd, needing still
signs and wonders, drained of memory

and you ask. Is my love surer
than the red rivers of calvary?

They asked which commandment is greatest
thinking: here shall we rank wickedness
and Christ!: love is first and last
a burnt offering of self
fouls the altar without love

for love is surer
than a carpenter night
nailing us to one tree.

So I exalt in you
who sieves night and day
with a silk cotton scarf
casting all that's left in your hands
into a night of cockcrows and calvary
if the morning will come without penitent tears.

But the cock may crow thrice, crow
till it be sore in the throat
my love will be surer than Thomas, Pilate, Caesar,
surer than the night's bleeding star.

3 May, 1992

(v) You sensed the terror of the times
(for M.)

I

We still walk the wilderness, held fast
to the terror of sandstorms and thirst
our tent, travelled by rivers, big and small
withers with crops for want of water
we powder the dirt of generations

with the dust of blind wanderings:
who treats boils and sores
where the cry of death is lone medication
for the dying? where streets
weep with deserted life? Simpler
to save energies for quiet sorrows
than work anger up to mountains of fire
for we die still, in a consummation redder
than all the blood of a smoking sea.

II

A theology of tears from the cabinet
sprays its seeds in the streets, aided
to vegetal growth by temperate winds,
scars of colonial wounds
are cold comfort to their festal reopening:
the serpent's second sting is lethal.
Tortured memory counselled double caution
on the puff-adder path of Bretton Woods,
tortured memory counselled new paths
sought to raise pulpits for a catechism of laughter
above the unholy theology of tears
scripted for a stage of broken bones—
which is why there is treason in a tongue
bespoken to a sharing of song or sorrow.

III

Beyond the ovation of dance halls
beyond the thrills of a passion
(in which the soul completely rejoiced)
the pirouetting toe became a question mark
to the logic of leisure on sated faces
whose claps of pleasure resounded
as rude slaps on the cheeks of those
for whom even sleep is torture.
It was time to seek new pastures
time to seek new valleys, wide

and full enough to banish an eternity
of want, where beside running waters
all could restore their souls and clap
ovation to their own dance of one love.

IV

Now you seek the patterns of another dance
the choreography of feet and limbs
tethered to giant pillars of living,
of limbs crushed by the strain of breaking stones
fetching cupfuls of sweat to kill thirst
and for this, you came across vast waters
bitter with a harsh history
but perhaps you too will break the bread
of sorrow and only then boast a full belly
with them whose table serves it as full menu
which also is why you bless the Arab child's stone
with the miracle of David's sling
storing hope in a prayer of perfect peace
to break the walls of profane battles.

V

You sensed the utter terror of the times
and built a castle of laughter for your soul
with it, you blunt the knife-edge dangers
of a chain-ganged existence:
"There is too much pain in the world", you said.
Now I declare to you that this earthquake
is me pouring the lava of my blood
to scour sins too deep for soap and water
this earthquake is me flowing into your bones
where fire and laughter seek to vanquish
cast-iron evils. But yours, you will agree
was the swallow's swoop to sip the sea
still I mark the bitter cup you tasted
for you came in a season of full brew.

27 July, 1992

(vi) The space you left behind

(for one who came, and naturally, left)

The space you left behind
is now a field of weeping willows
sadness spread to a wandering toe
is the nourishing tap root. I walk
this field in unfurled leafage, careful
not to multiply misery that mounts flowers
fearful of telling their hearts' secret colours
in a world shrouded in sham and shadow.

The space you left behind
heaves with the heaviness of land and water
which between us have stretched their arms
to plant acres of silence. I plod through
its vastness listening to the seconds,
to time so short, but long enough
to shed strange brows of their questioning brambles,
long enough to burnish sprouting hearts.

The space you left behind
has stretched itself into a street
which was the beginning. I greet
that street now with the spark of a fire
lit in handshake, your solar smile
night could not diminish, grown
in your fruitwine mouth, riper than all
the pears and pineapples of the orchard's prize harvest.

And I must put it down in this poem too
that the space you would leave behind sprouted me
who being artless save for the art of poetry
was the clumsy peasant, poet and schoolboy:
If I gave you my picture would you take it?
And I being so loud that night
you turned me out and cried, or the other
in which exulting in the warmth of water wells
I stirred false colours in your rising mind.

The space you left behind
has grown a forest of memories
which I cannot pluck from their heart-hidden place
to scatter about in stuttering words.
Now I wish same poetry that opens me
to ravages of deep longings
would unlock the road to your distant dance.

22 August, 1992

Nkiru (tomorrow's song)

I

You walk past
and a hoodlum with back on lamppost
sheaths his knife and prays for rebirth;
such is the power of your presence.
You pass the streets of red light
and turn the dry creek's starved leech
bleeding pools of alcohol
from the dizzy heads of drunkards,
cleaned of corruption
they discern virtue from your palm;
such is the power of your presence.

II

In a season of walking reeds
you announced once, a retreat to Otukpo.
I grew instantly, the fever of burning fields
in smoke-filled savannahs. You returned
smoothed over by the smile of life.
I have counted beyond seven lean years
beyond the widest ken of diviners' cowries,
I have counted decades of rot and ravage
but perhaps, this is tribute to your mystery
of flesh in a valley of bones? A prophecy of life
after this death is belled to your full hips.

III

What we long for lies in shores far removed
in an age though ripe is still unwombed,
only goats and goat-herds can best tell
the anguish of pasture in dry seasons
they can best tell what strengthens hoofs and feet
to seek meadows from sahels to sea shores.
Blessed are they that thirst after life
they shall drink aplenty from a hidden brook
beneath dense thickets in wooded forests
where its joys shall taste manifold
like wine, seasoned by the sojourner's aged search.

IV

I remember an evening of choruses
we had finished a rally, thumbed the air quite strong
with sufficient songs and slogans for our cause.
You came with Funmi, the energy
of change, flowing in gentle currents like rivers.
You both sang, lighting alive a photograph
lodged in my head that first night
when I beheld you in simple dress,
a bowl of home-made grains in your hand
humming a song like you always do.
My voice had frogged at the rally
but you sang so well that after you left, they said:
"she must be from God's choir!"

V

You boast the secret of growth in drought
to greater depths than baobabs,
you sum it up in a philosophy of work
admitting that here in our country
they plough and harvest for thieves' barns
who wear their palms thin to bone.
So lately, you lace your songs with sad refrains
sung to the memory of those that pad pain

with the worm-eaten wastes of harvest.
But a task is still undone:
the retrieval of stolen treasures,
its arduousness demands a new song
plaited to the early rays of tomorrow's song.

VI

I, like my country, have withered in the morning.
But you remain my mangrove ponds' water lilies,
they know not the strife of lean seasons;
you remain the song of all seasons:
men sweltering under a bitter yoke
sense your presence in a taste of water
and lap your song to sweating brows.
We need not cast cowries for this,
nor wait for the hollow auguries of government,
a prophecy of life after this death
is belled to your full hips.

VII

Come rest then on the crackling twigs of my arms
let them burst alive with new leaves,
let them be home to bird, fruit and flower
your songs shall be richer then
hitched to other choruses and the chants of children,
with your gentle stripes of faith
you will chase famine from my plundered temple
and nursed to life to match your freshness
we will fatten to the fullness of your hips
the frightfully lean shape of our land.

December, 1990